G. Dyer

Slavery and Famine

Punishments for sedition; or, an account of the miseries and starvation at Botany

Bay

G. Dyer

Slavery and Famine
Punishments for sedition; or, an account of the miseries and starvation at Botany Bay

ISBN/EAN: 9783741177606

Manufactured in Europe, USA, Canada, Australia, Japa

Cover: Foto ©ninafisch / pixelio.de

Manufactured and distributed by brebook publishing software
(www.brebook.com)

G. Dyer

Slavery and Famine

SLAVERY AND FAMINE,

PUNISHMENTS FOR SEDITION;

o r,

AN ACCOUNT

oF

NEW SOUTH WALES,

AND OF THE

MISERABLE STATE OF THE CONVICTS,

By GEORGE THOMPSON,

Who failed in the ROYAL ADMIRAL, May, 1792.

WITH SOME

PRELIMINARY REMARKS.

AND

A SKETCH OF THE CHARACTER OF

THOMAS FYSCHE PALMER, B. D. late Senior Fellow
of Queen's College, Cambridge.

By GEORGE DYER,

AUTHOR OF THE COMPLAINTS OF THE POOR PEOPLE
OF ENGLAND.

SECOND EDITION.

LONDON:

PRINTED FOR J. RIDGWAY, YORK STREET,
ST. JAMES'S SQUARE.

MDCCXCIV.

ADVERTISEMENT

TO THE

SECOND EDITION.

IT is my intention to pay a tribute of respect, more at large, elsewhere, to the other gentlemen, Muir, Margarot, Skirving, Sinclair, and Gerald, who have been convicted of Sedition. But my present engagements did not leave me sufficiently at leisure, to particularize what I meant to say of those sufferers. If this pamphlet should fall into the hands of any of their friends, I have to intreat them to impute my silence on the characters of those gentlemen to its true causes, viz. want of time, and want of information. For my part, I am not afraid to say, I feel great respect for them all, and I think them all alike entitled to the attention of the friends of liberty and humanity. To the insinuation thrown out in the House of Commons against Palmer, I think it

un-

PEOPLE

CALLED

QUAKERS.

THOUGH I am unconnected with your focieties, I have long been an admirer of your manners: though I may differ from you on fome religious and political quefions, I am charmed with your virtuous conduct. In thefe Preliminary Remarks will be found a fimplicity in the ufe of names, which though in itfelf, natural, may be deemed, by many, romantic ; and though coming from a child of peace, may even be thought to favour fedition. I addrefs this little work to you : it is a tribute of efteem : I exprefs refpect for your example : I feek protection from your alliance.

Long before that æra, at which the artificial difinctions of fociety may date their infignificance, they were deemed worfe than infignificant by me; they were deemed fo by you. With refpect to forms of government, indeed, fome of us, perhaps, may differ. But fhall it

be

be faid, that the men, who thinks thefe artificial diftinctions to be unnatural and injurious, muft be neceffarily republicans and levellers? William Penn was a friend to a limited monarchy. Shall it be faid that thofe who adopt the maxims of brethren are mere copyifts from others? When France was a nation of ariftocrats and flaves, ye were a fociety of friends.

Continue, ftill to bear your faithful teftimony. That example fhall produce, nay, has already produced, more conviction than all the reafonings of pride. France, that has been the firft to deride your theory, is become the firft to imitate your practice. But do not haftily fuppofe, that you have gained the fummit of wifdom. Your firft teachers gave you, on fome fubjects, folid information: on others, I think they mifled your judgment. What I deemed their miftakes, I have endeavoured to point out elfewhere, thinking it to be my duty, while acknowleging your merits, to difcharge my obligations *, by exercifing a liberty out of your focieties, which would not have been allowed me within them.

* See the Fourth Part of an Inquiry into the Nature of Subfcription to the Thirty nine Articles.

London, 10. of the third month, 1794.

PRELIMINARY REMARKS.

AFTER fo many circumftantial accounts of the fettlements in New
South Wales, the following fhort narrative
may appear to fome unneceffary, at leaft,
if not impertinent. The defign, therefore, of the publication of it, and the means
by which it fell into my poffeffion, together with fome obfervations connected with
the narrative, or arifing from correlative
circumftances, fhall be laid before the readers : fome indulgence may reafonably be
expected, as my inquiries have arifen
merely out of the fpur of the occafion:
method muft give way to matters of fact,
and elegance of language to accuracy of
ftatement.

B
When

When my esteemed friend T. Fysho Palmer was sent to the hulk at Woolwich, it was natural for me to pay him all the regards of friendship, and to feel an interest in his future fortunes; the same anxiety that I experienced for F. Palmer, I was soon led to feel for the amiable Thomas Muir; the same for the other worthy men, who are suffering alike in the cause of virtue, and equally entitled to the attention of their country.

Being one day on board the Staniflaus hulk, I heard the following narrative rehearsed; it immediately occurred to me that it should be made public; and I was afterwards pressed by some friends to undertake the publication myself—Little solicitation was necessary: I was happy to indulge at the same time the sympathies of friendship, and to obey the calls of humanity; and am now happy, after receiving information myself, to be enabled to gratify, at a small expence, the public curiosity. Having, therefore, obtained the
consent

confent of Thompfon's wife to publifh the narrative, and been commiffioned by a bookfeller to purchafe of her the copy, I have no doubt of performing an agreeable fervice to many readers.

The virtues, the talents, the learning, of the gentlemen mentioned above, have called forth no fmall degree of the public notice ; and I wifh my readers to know, that their patience and their fortitude are equal to their other virtues. The fituation of perfons thus circumftanced cannot be difgraceful, though it is certainly perilous ; they are fhortly to be tranfported to a country, where the horrors of famine may prefs upon thofe of flavery. Such perfons are entitled to fomething more than the public fympathy.

In the accounts given by different writers of thefe fettlements, fome confiderable variations are apt to occur. Nothing is more common than to read in the books of voyagers defcriptions fome-

what

what different of the fame people. It
fhould not therefore furprize the moft ex-
act readers to perceive, that Thompfon's
narrative varies in fome few particulars
from that of others. Captain Hunter
in his HISTORICAL ACCOUNT of PORT
JACKSON, and NORFOLK ISLAND, fpeaks of
the natives as a lively and ingenious people. Capt. Tench's defcription of them
too is fomewhat favourable in point of ingenuity. Thompfon, on the other hand,
fpeaks of them as exceedingly dull : the
fame character of dullnefs is alfo given
them in the account of the VOYAGE of
the ENDEAVOUR. Thompfon, I would obferve, did not ftay long at Port Jackfon ;
and it muft be confefled that the character
of a people cannot be afcertained from a
hafty furvey : in favages too, whofe minds
have admitted few ideas, whofe concep-
tions fo differ from our own, and whofe
manner of communicating them is fo liable
to miflead, precifion is ftill more difficult.
Captains Hunter and Tench have certainly been more converfant with the natives :
and

and may probably, therefore, be more accurate in their relation on some subjects, than Thompson, or even Capt. Cook. But I cannot forbear observing, that Thompson's representation of the natives of New South Wales, with regard to intellect, is very consistent with their ordinary practice of excessive eating, even to surfeiting and sickness ; and with various particulars related by other voyagers. Their general character, too, as exhibited by Thompson, accords, in my opinion, with the circumstances related by Hunter and others, as does their disposition towards the new settlers : As to the condition of the convicts, I think it probable, that Thompson's account may be more accurate than any other. In short, Thompson appears to me an ingenious and sensible young man, many of his observations carry marks of originality ; I, at least, have not met with them in other journalists : and they evidently wear the appearance of truth. Wherever I have thought him mistaken, I have taken the liberty of adding a note ; especially,

especially, as he seems not to have read
the Narratives of other voyagers *.

It will appear from the following account, compared with various particulars
related by others, that the New Settlement does actually lie exposed to danger
from famine. This will, therefore, be
the principal object of my confideration,
and I beg the reader's ferious attention to
the following references.—

* The Royal Admiral East Indiaman, in which
Thompson was Gunner, carried out 301 males, and
40 female convicts. He had the charge of thefe, as
also the care of the provifions, &c. Prefixed to
his Narrative is a lift of the Colonifts, Soldiers,
and Convicts, with the time of their conviction, &c.
together with a lift of the daily allowance of each
mefs, of fix perfons, and of the daily expenditure of
convicts from May, 1792, when the Royal Admiral
failed from Portfmouth, to October, when it arrived
at Port Jackfon. His Journal difcovers great attention, and I conclude him to be a very excellent fea-
man. He is at prefent Mate in a veffel that goes from
St. Helena to Denmark, but would fill a fuperior
ftation in the naval line with credit to himfelf, and
with advantage to the public.

Captain

Captain Tench refided at Port Jackfon almoft four years, viz. from the 20th of January, 1788, to the 18th of September, 1791. In April, 1790, he obferves as follows : " On the 17th inftant, the Supply, Captain Ball, failed for Batavia. We followed her with anxious eyes until fhe was no longer vifible. Truly did we fay to her, " *In te omnis domus inclinata recumbit.*" We were, however, confoled by reflecting, that every thing that zeal, fortitude, and feamanfhip, could produce, was concentered in her Commander.

" Our bofoms confequently became lefs perturbed ; and all our labour and attention were turned on one object—the procuring of food. Pride, pomp, and circumftances of glorious war were no more.

. " The diftrefs of the lower claffes for clothes, was almoft equal to their wants. The ftores had been long exhaufted, and winter was at hand. Nothing more ludicrous can be conceived than the expedient

ent of fubftituting, fhifting, and patch-.
ing, which ingenuity devifed, to eke out
wretchednefs, and preferve the remains of
decency. The fuperior dexterity of the
women was particularly confpicuous.
Many a guard have I feen mount, in which
the number of foldiers without fhoes, ex-
ceeded that which had yet preferved rem-
nants of leather.

" Nor was another part of our domeftic
economy lefs whimfical. If a lucky man,
who had knocked down a dinner with
his gun, or caught a fifh by angling from
the rocks, invited a neighbour to dine
with him, the invitation always ran,
" Bring your own bread." Even at the
Governor's table, this caution was conftantly obferved. Every man when he fat
down pulled his bread out of his pocket,
and laid it by his plate."

I have myfelf heard, by a gentleman immediately connected with Governor Phillip, that the Governor himfelf has fat
down

down to a fcanty allowance. Captain
Tench further obferves, in a note,
" Three or four inftances of perfons who
perifhed from want, have been related to
me. One only, however, fell within my
own obfervation. I was paffing the pro-
vifion-ftore, when a man, with a wild
haggard countenance, who had juft received his daily pittance to carry home,
came out. His faultering gait, and eager
devouring eye, led me to watch him;
and he had not proceeded ten fteps before
he fell. I ordered him to be carried to
the hofpital, where, when he arrived, he
was found dead. On opening the body,
the caufe of death was pronounced to be
inanition." It is in a high degree probable, nay, from various particulars to be
collected from different Journals, certain,
that many unhappy creatures muft have
perifhed from the fame caufe. Thompfon's account of thefe matters is, I doubt
not, in the main, true: the number, however, ftated by him to have died in one
year, through ficknefs, want of provi-

c   fion,

fion, hard labour, loathfome difeafe, or natural decay, may, probably, exceed matter
of fact. I have, therefore, left it blank *,
though I by no means think his relation improbable; apprehending, that his
account includes the returns of all the different fettlements I mean to compare,
and to afcertain, at my leifure, as accu-
ately as I can, the different ftatements
and probabilities relative to this fubject;
but wifh to leave it out of the power of
any reader to fay, that either Thompfon
or I have mifled him; at prefent, the
reafons for forwarding this work prevent
an immediate inveftigation. Thompfon
does not mention the precife year of this
calamitous event; it was probably near
the time of the lofs of the Sirius and
Guardian frigate.

* He makes it amount even to 1300.

I fhall

I fhall now lay before my readers, from well known voyagers, various obfervations on the foil, &c. of the new fettlements.— Captain Hunter in his HISTORICAL JOURNAL OF THE TRANSACTIONS AT PORT JACKSO NA ND NORFOLK ISLAND, obferves as follows, (p. 77.)

" As I have mentioned fomething of the country between Botany Bay and Port-Jackfon, I muft further obferve, that in the neighbourhood of Sydney Cove, which is that part of this harbour in which Governor Phillip has fixed his refidence, there are many fpots of tolerably good land, but they are in general of but fmall extent; exclufive of thofe particular fpots, it is rather a poor fteril foil, full of ftones; but near, and at the head of the harbour, there is a very confiderable extent of tolerable land, and which may be cultivated without waiting for its being cleared of wood; for the trees ftand very wide of

each

each other, and have no underwood: in short, the woods on the spot I am speaking of resemble a deer park, as much as if they had been intended for such a purpose, but the soil appears to me to be rather sandy and shallow, and will require much manure to improve it, which is here a very scarce article; however, there are people whose judgment may probably be better than mine, that think it good land; I confess that farming has never made any part of my studies. The grass upon it is about three feet high, very close and thick; probably farther back there may be very extensive tracts of this kind of country, but we, as yet, had no time to make very distant excursions into interior parts of this new world."

This was about eight months after they landed.

Captain

Captain Tench has given one of the lateſt hiſtories of this ſettlement, IN HIS COMPLETE ACCOUNT OF THE SETTLE- MENT AT PORT JACKSON, dated in his Journal November, 1790, in which he obſerves as follows of Sydney Cove,

" Cultivation, on a public ſcale, has for ſometime paſt been given up here, (Sydney) the crop of laſt year being ſo miſerable, as to deter from faither experi- ment ; in conſequence of which, the go- vernment farm is abandoned, and the people who were fixed on it, have been removed. Neceſſary public buildings advance faſt ; an excellent ſtorehouſe, of large dimenſions, built of bricks, and covered with tiles, is juſt completed, and another planned, which will ſhortly be begun. Other buildings, among which I heard the governor mention an hoſpital, and permanent barracks for the troops, may alſo be expected to ariſe ſoon. Works
of

of this nature are more expeditiously performed than heretofore, owing, I apprehend, to the superintendants lately arrived, who are placed over the convicts, and compel them to labour. The first difficulties of a new country being subdued, may also contribute to this comparative difficulty.

" Vegetables are scarce, although the summer is far advanced, owing to want of rain. I do not think that all the showers of the last four months put together, would make twenty-four hours rain. Our farms, what with this, and a poor soil, are in wretched condition. My winter crop of potatoes, which I planted in days of despair, (March and April last) turned out very badly, when I dug them about two months back. Wheat returned so poorly last harvest, that very little, besides Indian corn, has been sown this year. The Governor's wound is quite healed, and he feels no inconveniency whatever from it. With the natives we are hand and glove. They throng the camp every day, and sometimes

by

by their clamour and importunity for bread
and meat (of which they now all eat
greedily) are become very troublesome.
God knows, we have little enough for our-
selves! Full allowance (if eight pounds of
flour, and either seven pounds of beef, or
four pounds of pork, served alternately,
per week, without either peafe, oatmeal,
spirits, butter, or cheese, can be called so)
is yet kept up; but if the Dutch snow
does not arrive soon it must be shortened,
as the casks in the storehouse, I observed
yesterday, are woefully decreased."

Tench's Complete Account, &c. p. 73, 74.

Rose-

Rofe-Hill, or Paramatta, is the princi-
cipal fettlement, Captain Hunter remarks,

" After my arrival at Port Jackfon, I
went to Rofe-Hill, where great improve-
ments are carrying on ; a confiderable town
was laid out, many good buildings were
erected, and roads were cut, with about
two hundred and thirteen acres of land
cleared for corn, and eighty acres for buildings and gardens ; that is, the trees were
cut down, but the roots remained in the
ground, which would certainly leffen the
quantity of cleared ground : this ground
being grubbed up and laid open, gave me
an opportunity of examining what the foil
confifted of, and although I do not pretend
to any knowledge in farming, yet I thought
it required no very great judgment to perceive and determine this favourite fpot
(which, to do it juftice, is certainly better
than any upon or near this harbour) to be a
poor, fandy, fteril foil ; the furface is
covered

covered a few inches deep with a foil,
which feems to be produced from decayed
vegetation, rotten leaves, burnt and wi-
thered grafs; and under that is a mere
bed of fand.

" Rofe-Hill is certainly a pretty fituation, but the country will require much manure, much dreffing, and good farmers to
manage it, before good crops can be expected from it; the beft they have ever
had, I have been informed, has amounted
only to fix or feven to one, and this laft
feafon has been little more than two to
one, but that may in fome meafure be ac-
counted for by there being a great fcarcity
of rain.

" If it be the determination of Government to perfevere in eftablifhing a fettlement in this country upon an extenfive
plan, the nation muft be contented to
fubmit to a very heavy expence, It muft
be ftocked with cattle, were it only for
the manure, for without manure this

D   country

country is too poor ever to yield tolerable crops ; and if it fhould be refolved
upon to ftock it with cattle, it will be
found highly neceffary to employ a confiderable number of people in the care of
them, to prevent their being frequently
attacked by the natives, whom we know
are frequently driven to very great diftrefs
for food."

Hiftorical Account, &c. page 101, 102.

—————

Lieutenant King in his account of the
tranfaétions at Norfolk Ifland, in April
1788, obferves as follows :

" The wheat, which was fown in the
garden ground on the 2d was entirely eat
up with rats by the 4th; they did not
leave a fingle grain in the ground. As I
had no cats, and only one dog, thefe ver-
min were likely to prove a ferious nui-
fance ;

fance ; however, in order to rid ourfelves of them as much as poffible, I carried all the empty cafks to be converted into traps,"

Hunter's Hiftorical Journal, page 306.

Lieut. King adds, p. 311. " We now had two formidable enemies to encounter in the rat and grub-worm, both which were very numerous and deftruftive : fome wheat had been fown in the garden ground on the 11th, and the next morning there was not a grain of it left, being all cat up by the rats ; and the few potatoes and other vegetables, which efcaped the bad effects of the foutherly wind, were all eat up by the grub-worm. I have before ob-ferved, that on our firft difcovering the rats to be numerous, I ordered the empty cafks to be converted into traps, and for fome time they were very fuccefsful ; thirty or forty rats being caught for feve-ral nights together : thefe were killed and fcattered about the gardens, to deter the

reft

reft from coming to the place; but they foon grew too cunning to be caught in the traps, and too bold to be intimidated by their dead companions." The grain met with fimilar fate in June. Out of fix ewes, that Lieutenant King brought to the ifland, five died with the fcab. There are no animals in the ifland, but rats; and thefe, he obferves, are very deftructive, and very numerous. He, however, fays, they are now much thinned, and gave it as his opinion, in 1788, that they would be capable of fupporting themfelves in two years.

In Captain Tench's JOURNAL are to be read the following particulars:

" April 1791. Notwithſtanding the ſupplies which had recently arrived from Batavia, ſhort allowance was again proclaimed on the 2d of April, on which day we were reduced to the following ration :

" Three pounds of rice, three pounds of flour, and three pounds of pork, per week.

" It was ſingularly unfortunate that theſe retrenchments ſhould always happen when the gardens were moſt deſtitute of vegetables. A long drought had nearly exhauſted them. The hardſhips which we in conſequence ſuffered were great, but not comparable to what had been formerly experienced. Beſides, now we made ſure of ſhips arriving ſoon to diſpel our diſtreſs : whereas, heretofore, from having never heard from England, the hearts of men ſunk ;

funk ; and many had begun to doubt
whether it had not not been refolved to
try how long mifery might be endured
with refignation.

  " Notwithftanding the incompetency of
fo diminifhed a pirtance, the daily tafk of
the foldier and convict continued unal-
tered. I never contemplated the labours
of thefe men, without finding abundant
caufe of reflection on the miferies which
our nature can overcome. Let me for a
moment quit the cold tract of narrative:
—let me not fritter away by fervile adap-
tations thofe reflections, and the feelings
they gave birth to :—let me tranfcribe
them frefh as they arofe, ardent and generous, though hopelefs and romantic.—I
every day fee wretches pale with difeafe,
and wafted with famine, ftruggle againft
the horrors of their fituation. How
ftriking is the effect of fubordination !
how dreadful is the fear of punifhment !—
The allotted tafk is ftill performed, even
on the prefent reduced fubfiftence :—The
  :   black-

blackfmith fweats at the fultry forge; the
fawyer labours pent up in his pit, and the
hufbandman turns up the fterile glebe.—
Shall I again hear arguments multiplied to
violate truth and infult humanity!—Shall
I again be told that the fufferings of the
wretched Africans are indifpenfable for the
culture of our fugar colonies: that white
men are incapable of fuftaining the heat of
the climate!—I have been in the Weft Indies:—I have lived there. I know that it
is a rare inftance, for the mercury in the
thermometer to mount there above 90°;
and here I fcarcely pafs a week in fummer
without feeing it rife to 100°: fometimes
to 105; nay, beyond even that burning
altitude.

" But toil cannot be long fupported without adequate refrefhment. The firft ftep
in every community, which wifhes to preferve honefty, fhould be to fet the people
above want. The throes of hunger will
ever prove too powerful for integrity to
withftand: hence arofe a repetition of
petty

petty delinquences, which no vigilance could detect, and no juftice reach. Gardens were plundered ; provifions pilfered ; and the Indian corn ftolen from the fields, where it grew for public ufe. Various were the meafures adopted to check this depredatory fpirit. Criminal courts, either fiom the tedioufnefs of their procefs, or from the frequent efcape of culprits from their decifion, were feldomer convened than formerly. The Governor ordered convict offenders either to be chained together, or to wear fingly a large iron collar, with two fpikes projecting from it which effectually hindered the party from concealing it under his fhirt : and thus fhackled, they were compelled to perform their quota of work."

" Complete Account, p. 108, &c,

In the month of January, 1790, that is about two years after their arrival at Botany Bay, Captain Hunter gives the following awful relation :

" In

" In every company, the converfation turned upon the long expected arrivals from England, which we had been for fome time paft in daily expectation of, with a fupply of provifions; our ftore here was now in a very exhaufted ftate, much more fo than we ever expected it would have been ; for it was the general opinion, that I fhould the laft year, on my arrival at the Cape of Good Hope, have there met with ftore-fhips bound to this coun- try, as it was always underftood that the fettlement would never have been reduced lower than one year's provifions in ftore.

" We landed in the country with two years provifions, at leaft with what was fuppofed, when we failed from England, would be the cafe ; that time was now elapfed, yet we had not been vifited by any fhips from Europe, and we ftill had re- maining provifions at half allowance to laft until June. We all looked forward with hope for arrivals with a relief ; and that every affiftance neceffary for ftrangers

might

might be at hand, I offered, with a few
men from the Sirius, to go down to the
fouth head of the harbour, there to build
a lookout-houfe, and erect a flag-ftaff upon
the height, which might be feen from
the fea ; and which might alfo communi-
cate information of fhips in the offing to
the Governor at Sydney Cove. The Governor approved my propofals. I went
down with fix men, and was accompanied
by Mr. White and Mr. Worgan the fur-
geons of the fettlement and Sirius. We
erected a flag-ftaff, and lived in a tent for
ten days, in which we compleated a tolerably good houfe. At the end of ten days,
I was relieved by Mr. Bradley with a frefh
party."

Hift. Acc. p. 169, 170.

In chap. vii. p. 171, this narrative is thus
continued:

" In February, we began to look a little ferious on our difappointment of arrivals:

vals: we had not now more than provifions till June, at the allowance I have already mentioned.

" The Governor now faw a neceffity
for dividing the fettlement, and fignified his
intention that fuch divifion fhould take
place foon, by fending a certain number
of marines and convicts, under the command of Major Rofs, the Lieutenant-governor, to Norfolk Ifland; at which place
he underftood there were many refources,
which Port Jackfon, or the country round
it did not afford; and the gardens and cultivated lands here alfo would then be more
enjoyed by the remaining numbers: ac-
cordingly an arrangement took place, and
on the 26th of February, I received an order to prepare the Sirius for the fea, and
to embark the Lieutenant-governor with
one company of marines, and the officers,
baggage, and 186 convicts; in all, 221
perfons; with fuch a proportion of the remaining provifions and other ftores, as the
fettlement at that time could furnifh ; and

I was

I was directed to land them upon Norfolk
Island: Lieutenant Ball, commander of
his Majesty's armed tender Supply, was ordered under my command, and he also
embarked a company of marines, and
twenty convicts.

"In consequence of this deplorable
situation, on the 14th of May, the Officers composing the council met the Lieutenant-governor, agreeable to appointment,
and published the following orders:"—' At
' a meeting of the governor and council
' held to consider of the very exhausted
' state of the provisions in this settlement,
' and to consult upon what means are
' most proper to be pursued, in order to
' preserve life until such time as we may
' be relieved by some arrivals from En-
' gland, of which we have been so long
' in expectation, but probably disappoint-
' ed by some unfortunate accident having
' happened to the ships intended for this
' country.   The state of the provisions
' having been laid before the council, and
' the

' the alarming fituation of the fettlement
' having been taken into the moft ferious
' confideration, the following ratio of pro-
' vifions was unanimoufly refolved and or-
' dered to take place on Saturday the 15th
' inftant, viz.

' Flour—three pounds per week, for
' every grown perfon.

' Beef—one pound and an half per ditto;
' or, in lieu of the beef, 17 ounces of
' pork.

' Rice—one pound per ditto.

' Children above twelve months old,
' half the above ratio. Children under
' twelve months old, one pound and an
' half of flour and a pound of rice per
' week. In future, all crimes which may
' by any three Members of the council be
' confidered as not of a capital nature,
' will be punifhed at their difcretion, by
' a farther

' a farther reduction of the prefent allow-
' ance of provifions.'

"" At this particular feafon we had one
advantage, which, when that leaves us, will
reduce us to very great diftrefs ; I think, .
then, that many of the convicts (who are
indolent to aftonifhment, and who can,
and frequently do, eat at one meal what
they are allowed for a week) muft, when
the refource I am going to mention fails,
PERISH FOR WANT, OR SUFFER DEATH
FOR THE DEPREDATIONS THEY ARE SO
MUCH INCLINED, EVEN IN TIMES OF
PLENTY, TO COMMIT UPON OTHERS."

In Norfolk Ifland is a bird, called,
from its fingular advantage, the Bird of
Providence : but this fingular advantage
can only be enjoyed for a feafon : fifh,
too, as well as the tropic birds and gan-
nets, cannot be depended upon as a certain
refource.   Of the fifh, Captain Hunter
fays, page 183.   " I have feen the weather fo ftormy, and the furf fo high for

near a month together, that a boat could
not be launched more than twice during
that period, and then only for a few
hours ; and even when they had got out, ·
they would fometimes bring in a hundred
fifh of from two to four pounds weight,
and at other times only five or fix fifh ;
fo that this fupply was very uncertain and
very trifling, when it was confidered that
we were above 500 people."

Much having been faid concerning the
great fertility of Norfolk Ifland, I would
juft obferve, that let its fertility be what it
may, its extent is very fmall : and if cultivation fhould even anfwer the expectations
of Lieutenant King as expreffed to Governor Phillip, it would probably be only
capable of fupporting the perfons themfelves who refide there. I think it is only
five miles in breadth, and three in length.
I have been informed, too, that in Norfolk
Ifland there are two harvefts in the year ;
that the ground never lies fallow ; and that
there

there is great want of manure : If fo, the
ftrength of this land muſt be foon exhauſted.

WHITE's JOURNAL OF A VOYAGE TO
NEW SOUTH WALES, relates more particularly to the natural productions of
that country ; interſperſed, however, are
ſome uſeful remarks of another kind.
In Auguſt 1788, he obſerves as follows : "The Supply arrived from Norfolk Iſland, after a long and rough paſſage. She had landed, but neither in
apparent ſafety, nor with facility, the
ſtores which ſhe carried to that place :
and, upon the preſent occaſion, I am
forry to add, that the hazard of landing
and embarking 'from the little iſland is ſo
very great, that Mr. Cunningham, a
Midſhipman of the Sirius (who refided on
it with Lieutenant King, the Superinten-
dent) was loſt, with three ſeamen, in a
boat that was ſwamped by the ſurf, which
on every part of the coaſt runs high, and
beats againſt the ſhore with great vio-
lence :

lence ; fo that I much fear, from the difficulty of accefs, and its fituation, it never
will prove of any great confequence, although it promifed fome advantages, particularly in furnifhing us with pine trees,
which grow here to a fize nearly equal to
thofe of Norway. In the whole ifland
there is not a harbour capable of admitting .
even fo fmall a veffel as the Supply, and
the anchorage on every part of the coaft is
equally bad." Page 211, 212.

From all that I have had time to collect,
I cannot forbear making the following ad-
ditional remarks.——The climate of Port
Jackfon is allowed to be very falubrious,
though more favourable to the human
conftitution, than to vegetable or animal
production. Of the foil it has been ob-
ferved, " that a fpot eminently fruitful has
never yet been found ; that there are fpots
curfed with everlafting and unconquer-
able fterility, no body can deny." The

F   traveller

traveller looks in vain for thofe chearing
fprings, that blefs more fertile coun-
ties; the ftream of Sydney is faid to
be a mere drain of a morafs; and the
river, as it is called, at Paramatta, a
a creek, fcarcely entitled to the name of
a brook. The Hawkefbury or Nepeah is
the only frefh water river yet known to
exift in this country. It is, however, un-
reafonable to conclude, that in fuch extenfive regions, there fhould not be found
fome tracts of country, which, by proper
cultivation, may become fruitful.

But with refpect to the prefent ftate of
things, if the reader furvey Port Jackfon in
the maps of Captains Hunter or Tench, he
will perceive, that on the North it is fe-
parated from Broken Bay, on the South
from Botany; and that all the land between thofe bays, except a fmall portion
called the Kangaroo ground, is, at prefent,
defcribed as either fandy, fwampy, or
rocky, which have hitherto mocked labour, and defeated cultivation. The land
between

between Paramatta and that fpot, where the overflowings of the Hawkefbury ceafe, is the only tract yet difcovered, in which cultivation can be enfured for any courfe of years. The calculations and probabilities, therefore, to be made from length of time, impiovements in hufbandry, increafe of labour, and of ex-pence, ftill remain to be realized: the difficulties, too, and coft attending this fyf-tem of colonization, muft be very confide-rable. I have heard from gentlemen, who ought to be, and I doubt not are, well in-formed on the fubject, that every convict tranfported to New South Wales, has coft government, on an average, a thoufand pounds. A rich and flourifhing people, indeed, may well afford to make a coftly experiment, and fhould turn a deaf ear to the cold fpeculatift, who would warn them againft ploughing in the fea, and reaping defpair!

But I cannot perfuade myfelf yet to lay down my pen. From the whole of

the

the preceding remarks it is evident, that
thefe diftant colonies were not capable
of fupporting themfelves, as low down as
1790, and 1791. By the extract from
Thompfon alfo it appears, that they could
not fupport themfelves in 1793: for he
landed there in October 1792, and continued there, I think, about three months.
They muft then, of courfe, depend on
fupplies from Great Britain, Batavia, the
Cape of Good Hope, or the Eaft Indies.
The voyage from Great Britain is made
fometimes in five months, often in fix, feven, or even eight months. Capt. Hunter
went from Port Jackfon to the Cape of
Good Hope by Cape Horn, and returned
in 219 days, after a very perilous voyage
round the world, and was very near being
loft. The weftern courfe from Van Die-
man's Land to the Cape has never yet been
tried, and would, proba bly, from the ftrong
wefterly winds, prove a very long and
tedious voyage. From the preceding obfervations, too, it appears, that two veffels
have

have actually been wrecked *. At the fituation of perfons, whofe very exiftence is at
the mercy of winds and feas, whofe fupplies depend on the wafting of a fingle
blaft, on the fafe arrival of a fingle veffel,
I cannot help feeling alarm ! Whether,
indeed, any fhips are regularly ftationed on
thefe barren coafts I am not certain. If
this has not been, at any time, the cafe,
(and I have heard this afferted) government fhould at leaft provide in future.

It will, perhaps, be thought by fome
readers, that I have prefented them with an
inaccurate picture of New South Wales.
The picture may be dark, I acknowledge :
but it is, I believe, not inaccurate. Since I
have engaged in this inquiry, I have employed myfelf night and day to collect au-
thentic information from books ; and I have
ftudied precifion. The picture, therefore,
which I have drawn, I venture to fay, is

* The Sirius near Norfolk Ifland, and the Guardian Frigate on her paffage from England.

a true

a true reprefentation : and when I confider this new world as the future abode of my worthy friend, placed in a fituation, at which the heart of man revolts, a perfon of approved virtue, and of fincere religion, poffeffed of fuch talents, and of fuch attainments, as eminently qualify him to be the ornament and comfort of civilized life ; when I confider thefe things, I fay, I am not likely, it may be fuppofed, to fearch for the concealed delights of New South Wales, or to decorate a picture, in itfelf unpleafant, with the embellifhments of invention. Nor is my imagination to be quickened, when I confider the ftate of others ; when paffing from a confideration of the prefent fufferers, I take a general furvey of the fubject ; when I recollect on what flender crimes this dreadful fentence of tranfportation frequently attends ; that the new fettlements are to be confidered not merely as the land of flavery, but as the bourn, from whence fcarcely any convicts have returned. No provifion, I am told, is made for the return of convicts ;

and

and the paſſage, if I recollect rightly, coſts about twenty pounds.

Concerning the policy of ſettling a new Colony with convicts, I ſhall ſay but little. Lord Bacon * obſerves, " it is a ſhameful and unbleſſed thing to take the ſcum of people, and wicked condemned men, to be the people with whom you plant ; and not only ſo, but it ſpoileth the plantation : for they will ever look like rogues, and not fall to work, but be lazy, and do miſchief, and ſpend victuals, and be quickly weary, and then certify over to their country, to the diſcredit of the plantation.

" The people, wherewith you plant, ought to be gardeners, ploughmen, labourers, ſmiths, carpenters, joiners, fiſhermen, fowlers, with ſome few apothecaries, cooks, and bakers."

Whenever I have heard this queſtion agitated, ſays Captain Tench, ſince my

* Chancellor Bacon's Eſſays, p. 33. Of Plantations.

return to England, the cry of, What can we do with them ? Where elſe can they be ſent ? has ſilenced me, p. 163.

I have read with attention that part of governor Phillip's voyage, which treats on this ſubjeĉt : I went to be informed—I came away unconvinced.——To point out the defeĉt of our penal laws; the utility of penitentiary houſes ; the yet uncultivated ſtate of our northern Iſles; the unexplored mines ſaid to be in Britain; the prudence of converting our waſte lands into national property ; and of furniſhing means, by which thoſe who have heretofore been injurious to their country, may henceforth be rendered beneficial, would to many appear romantic, and to me, would, at preſent, be tedious. The die is caſt, and in playing a hazardous game, it is deemed prudent not to be too nice in calculations, or too apprehenſive about conſequences.—Let me, however, at leaſt, lift a warning voice, and remind an untoward claſs of readers of the title page

of

of this book *, FAMINE AND SLAVERY, THE PUNISHMENT FOR SEDITION.

But doubtlefs not only thofe who planned, but thofe who have been delegated to execute an enterprize of fuch magnitude, have deeply revolved that great national expence does not imply the neceffity of national fuffering. While revenue is employed with fuccefs to fome valuable end the profits of every adventure being more than fufficient to repay its cofts, the public fhould gain, and its refources fhould multiply.—But an expence whether fuftained at home or abroad; whether a wafte of the prefent, or an anticipation of the future revenue; if it bring no adequate return, is to be reckoned among the caufes of national ruin †."

* For the title page I am indebted to a friend.

† Fergufon's Effay on the Hiftory of Civil Society, quoted by Capt. Tench.

POSTSCRIPT.

AS the fmall fketch drawn above, was
I own, the effect of fympathetic
friendfhip, it will not be thought out of
character to drop a word relative to my
friend. Thomas Fyfche Palmer, B. D. late
fenior Fellow of Queen's College, Cambridge, is of a refpectable and ancient family
at Ickwell, in Bedfordfhire ; was educated
at Eton School ; was entered at Queen's
College, Cambridge, and, after going
through the ftudies of the Univerfity with
credit, was chofen Fellow of that College.
He was ordained a clergyman of the efta-
bliſhed

blifhed church, and from the nature of
his connections, as well as the direction of
his ftudies, muft have had profpects of
confiderable preferment.   .

At Cambridge, Fyfche Palmer was a regular attendant on the Theological Lec-
tures of the late celebrated John Jebb,
though antecedently to this connection, he
had been of the calviniftic perfuafion, intimate with John Berridge and Rowland
Hill, two eminent methodift preachers of
the eftablifhed church. From an affiduous
and critical ftudy of the fcriptures he became
an unitarian, and poffeffing great activity of
mind, he then fhewed the fame zeal in
propagating the unitarian, as he had before
the trinitarian doctrines. He never held
any preferment.

Hearing of a fociety of unitarians formed at Montrofe by Thomas Chriftie, author of an excellent volume of Sermons
on the unity, Fyfche Palmer was induced to

go to Scotland, with a view of joining that
fociety. There he became a zealous teacher, formed unitarian focieties at Dundee
and Edinburgh, and taught occafionally in
feveral villages, particularly, in Forfar, and
Newborough. He never received any pay :
The employment of a teacher he thought
honourable, and ufeful ; but had long fince
laid afide the profeffion and garb of a
prieft.

Of his income derived from his fellow-
fhip and private fortune he devoted more
than half to benevolent purpofes : he was
a great economift, only to enable himfelf
to be a philanthropift.

The regulations of the focieties in which
F. Palmer taught were different from that
in many others. When I was lamenting in
his company the lofs which his fociety
would fuftain, he replied, " my friends will
feel little inconvenience from my abfence ;
they did not depend wholly on me ; they
will

will be capable of inftructing one an‑
other."

James Ellis, the young man gone with
him to Botany Bay, was formerly his fer‑
vant ; but proving himfelf to be a youth of
virtuous principles, and good talents, F.
Palmer took pains in giving him inftruc‑
tion ; and made him his companion.
James Ellis ufed to preach for him occa‑
fionally.

F. Palmer is not merely a man of
letters ? he is a man of exquifite tafte in
the fine arts, in painting, poetry and mu‑
fic, and poffeffes an excellent judgment in
architecture, gardening and hufbandry.
In the caft of his mind there is great origi‑
nality. He can be as ferious as any man ;
but he is likewife a mafter of humour. ‑
I know no character more upright ; few
more interefting. There will be fhortly
publifhed, by a fkilful hand, a more ample
account of this gentleman, together with
his

his Eſſays written in the Theological Re-
poſitory, and a Controverſial Treatiſe of
his, publiſhed ſome time ſince, on the Unity of God.—To ſay more concerning his
religious ſentiments would be quite foreign
to the nature of this Work, nor ſhould I;
indeed, have even touched on that ſub-
ject here, but with a view to exhibit the
real character of my friend.

With reſpect to the other gentlemen,
not being poſſeſſed of much original information, I can ſay but little: To the
abilities, learning, and worth of Thomas
Muir, all who have the pleaſure of his
acquaintance can bear teſtimony. He was
educated at the Univerſity of Glaſgow,
in Scotland; and from his diſtinguiſhed
talents would probably have been very
eminent as an advocate. The other gentlemen are poſſeſſed of reſpectable talents;
and few worthier characters, I am told
are to be found, than William Skirving.—

The

The proceedings on thefe trials have been thought illegal by fome of our firft lawyers: the fentences, therefore, will be, probably rejudged by pofterity; and when the fentences paffed by the Scotch judges are approved, the humanity of Henry Dundas will not be forgotten.

O D E,

'MIDST howling winds, and foaming deeps,
  No fear the guiltless suff'rer knows;
Peaceful amidst the storm he sleeps,
  Fearless to unknown regions goes.

The guilt that makes e'en tyrants groan,
  Dares not invade the patriots breast;
The prisoner feels himself his own,
  And triumph's most, when most oppress'd.

The bark that bears to barren lands
  And barb'rous tribes a prize so dear,
Shall keep it safe from ruffian hands,
  Or yield it to a nation's prayer.

Go, generous band, where honour calls,
  Your chains are virtue's fairest prize,
Who nobly lives, and nobly falls
  Stands but a step below the skies.

And thou, pure heart, shalt often send
  The ardent prayer to heaven for me:
And grateful still I call thee friend,
  And chearful would I follow thee.

EXTRACT

FROM THE

JOURNAL OF G. THOMPSON.

THE land of New South Wales, from Botany Bay to Port Jackfon, has a level appearance at firft fight, and may be feen at about the diftance of feven or eight leagues. As you come nearer, it appears hilly up the country, and full of trees. The entrance of the harbour is formed by two heads, called the North and South Heads, lying nearly in thofe directions, and

B   about

about three quarters of a mile diftant from each other. Juft within the Heads, and in the middle of the harbour, is a fhoal, with about four fathom water upon it at fpring ebbs ; in the channel about fifteen fathom ; it gradually fhoals as you get farther up. The whole abounds with iflands, coves, creeks, and harbours, up to Sydney, which is about nine * miles from the entrance, and makes the moft complete harbour in the univerfe : there your fhips lay within fifty yards of the fhore, in five fathom and a half, and as fmooth as in a fifh-pond. From Sydney Cove the harbour takes its courfe to Rofe Hill (or Parramatta). There is water up at low water for a large long boat ; the tide flows about eight feet at neap tides, and ten feet at the fpring, with very little ftrength.

* Governor Phillip makes Sydney Cove about five or fix miles from the entrance into the harbour ; the harbour alfo muft be more than three quarters of a mile acrofs, according to Phillip and White ; in other refpects Thompfon's account agrees tolerably well with theirs.

The harbour abounds with a variety of fish, most of them unknown in England; here is plenty of oyfters, cockles, and other shell fish. The best fish that are caught are snappers, mullets, light-horseman, (so called from their head resembling much a light-horseman's cap) flat-heads, salmon, whitings, and there are many other kinds of fish too tedious to mention.

Sydney is the spot where the first settlement was formed, merely for the advantage of good water, and the conveniency of the harbour. In this part are only gardens sufficient to supply the inhabitants with vegetables, &c. The Governor and principal officers chiefly reside here, and as many convicts as are sufficient to attend the store-houses, fishing-boats, different officers, &c. Those whose sentence is expired and are in expectation of getting home *, chiefly choose this place for their residence.

* None worth mentioning have ever returned.

About

About two miles from this place are the brick fields, where a great number of bricks and tiles have been lately made, but they are still in great want of lime-stone, or a substitute for it. At present a stiff kind of clay is used to build with, but it is such a weak cement they dare not attempt to raise their houses even one story. There is not such a thing on the colony as a set of stairs, except in the Governor's house, which is only one story, and is built with lime brought from England. The bricks and tiles are both of one colour, of a light brown, which make the buildings quite romantic. Those that are built of wood are white-washed with pipe clay, which is found here in great plenty.

Parramatta is the grand settlement, about sixteen miles from Sydney by land, the buildings are the same as at that place, forming one large street, nearly one mile long. The houses are all separate from one-another, space being left to enlarge them when

when neceſſary. There is a large hoſpital, church, ſtore-houſes, &c. The Governor has a houſe here upon Roſe Hill, a moſt delightful ſpot; here is a large park, called Cumberland Park, where the government cattle are put to graze: the greateſt part of the cattle and ſheep belonging to different people are at this place. There is at preſent about 100 acres of corn ſtanding here, chiefly Indian corn, ſome wheat, oats, barley, &c. They look remarkably well, and there is not the leaſt doubt of its being the moſt fruitful harveſt the colony has ever experienced. It will commence in about eight or ten weeks.

About four miles from this place is another ſettlement, Toongabby, where the greateſt number of convicts are, and work very hard, (there is alſo a good crop of corn ſtanding and promiſes well) their hours for work are from five in the morning till eleven *, they then leave off till two in the afternoon, and work from that time till ſun-

* Capt. Tench ſays till ten.

ſet.

set. They are allowed no breakfaſt hour, becauſe they have ſeldom any thing to eat. Their labour is felling trees, digging up the ſtumps*, rooting up the ſhrubs and graſs, turning up the ground with ſpades or hoes, and carrying the timber to convenient places. From the heat of the ſun, the ſhort allowance of proviſion, and the ill treatment they receive from a ſet of merciless wretches (moſt of them of their own deſcription) who are their ſuperintendants, their lives are rendered truly miſerable. At night they are placed in a hut, perhaps 14, 16, or 18 together (with one woman, whoſe duty is to keep it clean, and provide victuals for the men while at work) without the comforts of either beds or blankets, unleſs they take them from the ſhip they come out in, or are rich enough to purchaſe them when they come on ſhore. They have neither bowl, plate, ſpoon, or

* This may, perhaps, be done now; but when Capt. Tench was there, it is obſerved in his Journal, Nov. 16, 1790, "As all the trees on our cleared ground, were cut down, and not grubbed up, the roots and ſtumps remain,"

knife,

knife, but what they make of the green
wood of this country : only one small iron
pot being allowed to dress their poor allowance of meat, rice, &c. In short, all the
neceſſary conveniences of life they are
ſtrangers to, and ſuffer every thing they
could dread in their ſentence of tranſportation. Some time ſince, it was not uncom-
mon for ſeven or eight to die in one day, and
very often while at work, they being kept
in the field till the laſt moment, and frequently while being carried to the hoſpital ;
many a one has died ſtanding at the door
of the ſtore-houſe, waiting for his allowance of proviſion, merely for want of ſuſ-
tenance and neceſſary food. So great was
the mortality among them that upwards of
    died in one year ; and of 450 that
came from England in the Pitt *, only 29
were alive ſix weeks ſince at a general
muſter. Thoſe that are now living chiefly

* The Pitt ſailed in May 1791, and returned in
1793.—I think I have heard that ſome of theſe convicts went to Norfolk Iſland ; and ought to be deducted
from this account.

- owe

owe their lives to thofe that are dead, the provifion being fo fcarce, that had they not died all muft have perifhed. When our fhip arrived (which was quite unexpected) there was no more than one week's falt provifion in the ftore at the full allowance, which would have been reduced to one-third on the following week.

The women have a more comfortable life than the men ; thofe who are not fortunate enough to be .felected for wives, (which every officer, fettler, and foldier is entitled to, and few are without) are made hut-keepers : thofe who are not dignified with this office, are fet to make fhirts, frocks, trowfers, &c. for the men, at a certain number per day ; occafionally to pick. grafs in the fields, and for a very flight offence are kept conftantly at work the fame as the men. It is abfolutely neceffary to keep a ftrict difcipline among fuch people, and their punifhments are very fevere. The colony is by no means without good laws and officers of juftice ;
there

there is a judge, juſtice of the peace, and
conſtables, moſt of the latter are convicts.
At this time Barrington holds the poſt of
head conſtable at Parramatta, and is a very
diligent officer. For a very trifling offence
a convict is put into the ſtocks until it is
convenient to examine him; if guilty, he is
taken to a cart wheel to receive a Botany Bay
dozen, which is twenty-five laſhes ; if the
crime is ſuch as would be puniſhed by a
dozen on board a ſhip, or on ſhore in England, it is here puniſhed with two or
three hundred ; if it is any thing of conſequence, ſuch as theft, they are tried by a
regular court, which generally terminates
in a ſentence of death, or a ſecond tranſportation to Norfolk Iſland for life. At
the ſame time the convicts have the advantage of the laws as well as others.
No perſon, unleſs thoſe immediately con-
cerned with them, is allowed to ſtrike
them, or by any means ill uſe them ; all
complaints muſt be made to the juſtice,
who muſt be conſulted on the moſt trifling
occaſion.

The

10

The natives of New South Wales are not very numerous * : towards the sea coast they are quite black, of the middle size, and in general well limbed, have large flat noses, thick lips, and short hair, not of the woolly kind like the African negroes. They are a lazy indolent people and of no ingenuity. They never even think of seeking for food till hunger presses them ; their chief living is fish, which they catch with a hook and line, or with a fish gig made of wood and sharpened with fish bones or kangaroo teeth ; they have no other method of cooking but roasting the fish on the fire, which is generally done as soon as they get them out of the water : and they are frequently so hungry as not to allow themselves time to dress them, but eat them half raw : they commonly fish and eat till they can scarcely move † ; they then

go

* Capt. Hunter seems to intimate they are numerous ; though I think by his own Historical Journal it appears that they are not so, as well as from the Accounts of others.

† Capt. Tench observes of Colbee, "that a large dish

of

go on fhore, make a fire, and lay down to
fleep by the fide of it. They have no kind
of cloathing; both men and women are always naked: if it rains they fly to fome
hollow rock or cavern for fhelter: if it is
fine, they juft pull up fome long grafs,
make a fire, dry it and go to fleep on it.
They cannot bear to be confined to a hut
or tent. The Governor has built a very
neat brick hut for one of the Chiefs,. but
neither he or his family will live in it: they
will fometimes ftay at the place for a
day, then make a fire on the outfide of it.
In fhort, they prefer living in the woods
and going naked to the beft houfe or
clothes on the Colony. There are many
of them that vifit Sydney every day for
the fake of what they can get to eat, and at
night they return to the woods. There are
three or four of the Chiefs who attend the
Governor's houfe every day for their dinner and a glafs of wine. Several of the

of fifh was fet before him: he devour:d a *light horfe-
man*, and at leaft five pounds of beef and bread, even
till the fight of food became difgufting to him, p. 97.

officers

officers have both boys and girls as fer-
vants, but they are fo lazy that it is with
difficulty you can perfuade them to get
themfelves a drink of water: if you attempt to ftrike them, they will immediately fet out for the woods and ftay four
or five days. Indeed it is common for
them to ftrip-off what clothes they may
have on, and take a trip to the woods,
whether offended or not. If they were
fhy at the firft fettling in the Colony,
that is not the cafe now. For the people
can fcarcely keep them out of their houfes
in day time; at the fame time, they muft
be cautious how they affront them; if they
offend them, at the firft opportunity they
will certainly fpear them, at which they
are very dexterous *. Their fpears aro
made of the ftem of the grafs tree, are
about twelve or fourteen feet long, pointed
with fifh bone or teeth, and bearded with
fhells, ftuck on with gum, and are very

* In 1790 Governor Phillip obferves, that no lefs
than feventeen of our people had either been killed or
wounded by their fpears.

dangerous

dangerous weapons; they will throw
them fifty or fixty yards*, and ftrike within
two or three inches at a certainty; they
are very treacherous and deceiving: if they
chance to meet any perfon in the woods
fingly, it is ten to one but they fpear him
and ftrip him of his clothes, though of no
ufe to them; if there are two or three
together, they will not attempt to affault
them, particularly if they have a mufket,
at which they are much frightened: few
people travel the woods without one.
Some time fince one of them fpeared the
Governor quite through the fhoulder from
near the back bone to the neck, which
went through above five inches. He had .
one of their Chiefs with him at his houfe
fometime, and fearing he would go away,
had made him a prifoner: however, he
made his efcape; the Governor hearing
where he went, next day went about feven
miles from Sydney and found him and fe-

* He might have faid 60 or 70: Capt. Hunter
fays, I have fince feen a ftrong young man throw the
lance full ninety yards.

veral

veral more together; to convince them
he did not intend them any harm, he went
to them by himfelf, and while he was
expoftulating with this Chief, and intreat-
ing him to return, one of them who was
behind, ftruck him with the fpear and ran
away to the woods: but he fuffered fe-
verely for the offence, as foon as he was
found by the reft, they beat him in a moft
unmerciful manner, knocked one of his
eyes out, and nearly deprived him of life.
While the Governor was carried home
with the fpear in his fhoulder, which,
however, was not attended with any bad
confequence, in lefs than three weeks he
was able to walk out; they are divided into feveral tribes or cafts, and are known
to which they belong by the lofs of one of
their fore teeth, or the joint of their fore
or little finger * ; they have frequent wars
and defperate battles with each other at
fixed times; whenever a difpute arifes be-

* This feems probable. Captains Hunter and
Tench obferve, that as yet they had not been able
to difcover the caufe of thefe defects.

twcen

tween them that caufes a fight, they namo a certain day and fix a place to meet for the engagement : every one is armed with his fpear, a large club, ftone hatchet and a fhield ; they are at great pains to paint themfelves and make the moft terrible appearance they can at thofe times ; thofe who fall in the battle are left lying on the ground, without any more notice, except it be a Chief or fome one much refpected : then they cover him with wood, fet fire to it until the flefh is burnt from the bones, and in this ftate they leave it. Thofe that die naturally are not buried, but are left where they die, unlefs they be of note, then they are burnt ; they cannot bear the idea of dying by a natural death, which is indeed feldom the cafe, their frequent wars not fuffering them to live to a great age ; the oldeft that I remember to have feen, did not to appearance exceed thirty years *. If one of a family dies, they generally put

* Though in general they are not long lived, yet fome are known to live till fifty or fixty years of age.

one or more of the furvivors to death, and
a family of eight or nine has been often
known to be reduced to two or three in
the courfe of a month ; thefe two caufes
prevent their being numerous. They are
very quick in learning to fpeak Englifh,
and will repeat any fentence after you immediately, particularly any tune: when in
their canoes they keep conftantly finging
while they paddle along ; they have the
French tune of Malbrook very perfect : I
have heard a dozen or twenty finging it
together.

The different kinds of beafts, birds and
infects are numerous, and the birds in general are very beautiful : there is a great
variety of different forts of parrots, parro-
quetts, and many other birds unknown
in England, a great many infects alfo,
which are very troublefome and deftructive, one in particular that in the hot
dry feafon deftroys the corn : thefe have
been known to overfpread a field of corn
in the courfe of one night, and totally de-
ftroy

ftroy it. The musquittoes and flies are in great quantities: the latter will infect fresh meat in such a manner that it is sometimes difficult to keep it free from maggots even one hour after it is killed. Of the beasts the kangaroo is found to be the best eating, exactly resembling venison; they are sometimes shot and sometimes taken with dogs: in dry weather it is difficult to get them any way, owing to their swiftness in leaping; but in rainy and wet weather they are easily caught or shot; they often wound the dogs in a desperate manner with their tail, with which they strike with great force: they grow very slowly and are near two years before they come to their full size, and then they will weigh about 2 cwt. * they have a false belly in which they secure their young when pursued, and commonly carry them till they are five or six months old. There are a great many oppossums and flying squirrels which are good eating. Guanas,

* This circumstance is worth mentioning, that at its birth, the kangaroo is not so large as a full grown mouse.

snakes,

fnakes, &c. are very plentiful; there are
alfo fome of the fineft dogs wild in the
woods, and many other kind of beafts, but
none of them in the leaft dangerous.

The trees with which the whole country
abounds are found to be of little ufe, not
fit either for building houfes or boats,
though there are many boats built with
them, but they will not laft long, and likewife houfes, for neceffity has no law.
There are two kinds of oak, called the he
and the fhe oak, but not to be compared
with Englifh oak; and a kind of pine and
mahogany, fo heavy that fcarce either of
them will fwim. Some diftance up the
country the trees grow very ftrait, and to
a great heighth, though not one in a hundred are found. As an inftance, when
the Supply was ordered for England, fhe
wanted a new foremaft, and to find one to
anfwer fuch a fmall fhip, it coft them upwards of three weeks labour, in which time
they cut down more than thirty trees, before one was found to be found at the heart,
and

and this of fuch a weight, it was with difficulty they moved and erected it ; thero
are trees which produce two forts of gum,
a yellow kind which the natives make ufe
of for their fpears, fifh gigs and canoes ;
and a kind which is called dragon's blood,
but they are of no ufe but for the fire.

Here ends the ingenious narrative of
Geo. Thompfon, written, indeed, without
any view to publication ; the obfervations,
however, of a perfon, to whom the officers
on board the veffel * bear teftimony, that
his veracity may be depended on.

As an illuftration of fome reflections in
my Preliminary Remarks on the fevere
fentences inflicted for flight offences, I beg
leave to fubjoin the following hints.

A perfon in Kent about ten years ago,
lent a farmer a team of horfes, and fent a

* The Staniflaus hulk.

fervant

fervant with them. The horſes were worked hard, and had nothing to eat. The fervant took ſome corn out of a bin, to feed them with : this man was ſentenced at Maidſtone Affizes to ſeven years' tranſportation, and is, I believe, now at Botany Bay.

Edward Moſely was condemned by Judge Gould at Maidſtone in 1792, for ſtealing a game cock, to ſeven years tranſportation : he is now on board the Staniſlaus, unlefs gone with the other convicts in the Surprize.

On board the other hulks is, at leaſt, was, when I viſited the excellent Thomas Muir, a youth whoſe amiable deportment engaged the notice of the officers. A diſciple of Lavater looking at his countenance, would have ſaid, this youth cannot poſſeſs a vicious heart : he was obſerved to keep aloof from the other convicts, as not accuſtomed to their maxims, and when above deck, walked penſively

fively by himfelf; his crime I am informed was this: he had been in a fquab-
ble with a girl of the town, and whether
in a frolic, which I think was the cafe,
or not, he took her handkerchief: this
was faid not to be worth fixpence : it
was, however, valued at eleven pence, in
order to get a fentence fixed: the youth was
adjudged to feven years tranfportation.

The following cafe reflects great honour on the humanity of Captain Er-
fkine, of the Staniflaus hulk. A man in
Cornwall ftole a game cock, which was
found in his father's cuftody. The Juf-
tices of the Quarter Seffions fent both
father and fon for three years hard labour on the hulks; the father died of a
broken heart in a month. Captain Er-
fkine wrote to the Secretary of State
on the iniquity of the cafe. The fon
was pardoned.

Montrieul (Count) borrowed a fum of
money of Broughton, (Sir Thomas) to go

to Ireland. Montrieul altered his inten‑
tion and took another courſe. Brough‑
ton had him taken up for a ſwindler,
and by the juſtices of Suſſex he was ſen‑
tenced to three years hard labour on the
bulks.

Moſt of theſe caſes I received from
my benevolent friend ; who in commiſ‑
ſerating the ſevere ſentences of others,
forgot the ſeverity of his own.

In George Thompſon's liſt of con‑
vićts conſigned to New South Wales,
on board the Royal Admiral in 1792, are
the following : The reader will pleaſe to
notice the age of the convićt, and the term
of convićtion : Alexander Dempſter, aged
fifteen, labourer, received May 15, con‑
vićted Sept. 13, 1790, term of convićtion,
ſeven years : Stephen Peachman, nineteen
years of age, tranſported for life : Wil‑
liam Collins, Thomas Galloway, and
William Wales, each fifteen years of age,
tranſported for ſeven : Ann Wilſon, eigh‑
teen

teen years of age : Ann Holmes only fix-
teen, tranfported for life : and —— Scott,
only thirteen years of age, *(quis talia
fando temperet e lachrymis?)* TRANS-
PORTED FOR LIFE—!!

F I N I S.

ERRATUM.

Page 2 of Preliminary Remarks, *for* Fyche, *read*
Fytche.